RANSOM KHANYE

The Lamp and Light

Uncovering from history the foolproof prophetic future from the Bible

Cover design by Ransom Khanye

raniekaysbooks@gmail.com

ISBN 978-606-97233-11-1

Also available on Amazon by the same author:
He Never Left Me Alone
The Magic Oil: Unleashing the Power of Nature's Remedy - Castor Oil
The Magic Oil 2: More Castor Oil Miracles
Amazing Natural Remedies: Nature's Medicine Cabinet

Acknowledgements

This booklet would not be what it is without the dedicated help of a few friends who helped me spot a good number of typos and ambiguities. I am grateful for the time they spent combing through it and pointing out the mistakes which were not so obvious to me in my reading. I hope that whatever was not spotted, if anything, will be minimalistic and not affect the overall content and contexts of the booklet much. As such I want to say thank you to:
Maureen York
Everton Hartley
Lori Veal-Yerxa

I also want to thank *Ivor Myers* for letting me use much of his sanctuary message as a major part of my content in this booklet from the Youtube video titled the G.P.S. God's Plan of Salvation.

FOREWORD

This booklet contains some of the most amazing fulfilled prophecies that are found in the Bible. There are a lot of people who are sceptical about the Bible and who call it an ordinary book that was written by human beings. This booklet should convince anyone that the Bible is no ordinary book. It is not a human project but God's very own project that was put together by inspired human beings. God works through human beings to reach other people and the things that God has written in the Bible are things that you just cannot make up. As you delve into this booklet you will find proofs of the inerrancy of the Bible in museums, history books and archaeology. You will discover that the coherence and accuracy of the events in the world and their Biblical foretelling is the very proof you have always sought to convince you to trust in the divinity of the Bible and hence in the God of the Bible.

The Bible is the only book that you will ever need to read to learn about God. This booklet is just here to show you that the Bible is worth your consideration and concentration. May the God of the Bible, the creator of the universe, richly bless you.

Contents

1 MODERN EVENTS INVOKE BIBLE REFLECTION AND NOSTALGIA

And he causeth all, both small and great, rich and poor, free and bond, to receive a mark in their right hand, or in their foreheads:
And that no man might buy or sell, save he that had the mark, or the name of the beast, or the number of his name. (Revelation 13:16-17)

As the Democratic party of the United States of America proposed a bill to help avert an economic disaster resulting from the closure of borders and schools and sporting events and institutions in general, the idea sent shockwaves through the cryptocurrency world, known just as Bitcoin mining by many.

Something else seemed to be taking shape though. The piece of the puzzle that I have always wondered about: how the buying and selling referred to in Revelation 13 was going to be restricted to those who accept the mark of the beast.

History is full of things that did not at first appear possible when first prophesied. Shortly we must unpack these history fulfilled prophetic facts. Indeed, it is extremely difficult to see the forest from the trees when they first appear.

Credit cards and bank debit cards appeared as the most probable vehicle for heralding the cashless society. Then it seemed as if that would not really work because the poor people and those in the third world will always need to use cash. So perhaps panicking about the mark of the beast via payment cards was amiss. I think they are just part of a bigger picture and so it is reasonable to keep them in focus.

Tesco, the UK supermarket giant with shops also in Hungary, has a customer loyalty program. They issue points for every pound spent against the customer's "club card". The other thing that the club card does is link the purchases to the customer's identification details as saved on Tesco's computer systems. This way they have a record of purchasing habits and each item the customer has ever bought with the card in use is kept on a database. As a reward the customer gets cash vouchers back periodically. This serves as a cheaper way for targeted marketing by Tesco since they then have a full profile of the customer's spending habits. Sainsbury's supermarket is the same with their "nectar" points issued against each pound spent.

The fairly recently introduced "scan as you shop" option firstly by Tesco and now also by ASDA supermarket has a way to do shopping using a barcode scanner as the customer collects every item from the shelves. The advantage of this is that the customer can pack their shopping into their bags and then just pay on their way out without having to take the items out of the bag or the trolley again. Lately Tesco has disabled the use of cash in their scan as you shop option. That means all the "scan as you shop" customers must now pay by card. At the same time facial recognition self-checkouts have suddenly shown up in ASDA supermarkets' self checkout tills.

In countries where cards have not been issued to as many people as those who spend money, mobile phones have. Mobile phone usage has exponentially expanded globally. With this expanded use has come the ease with which financial transactions can be made without the use of cash. This makes it possible for those in the global diaspora to send funds to almost anyone and anywhere in the world. The money sent can be spent by the people who receive it without even a coin or note of cash being touched by anyone in the entire transaction.

So global cashlessness is not an impossible thing nowadays. What brings the idea of cashlessness back into focus is the fact that lately we are now constantly hearing of and seeing signposts about the need to distance ourselves and be metres apart. There is also a need to use hand sanitiser and also to wear gloves and masks. We were even being told that the corona virus was being spread by touching petrol pumps (could this mean it is better where attendants pour fuel for us as they still do in Africa?).

The implementation of the restriction of buying and selling stated in the Bible cannot be too far off. It may be that the apparent US digital dollar will set the trend for the different world governments to implement digital currencies too. Until now the digital currencies have not been used by governments and the cryptocurrency world has remained a domain of just part of the global population, though growing in number. To think that this is definitively the way things are going may be right, but we cannot be so certain for now. Yet we must not be taken by surprise when it does happen. With all the cashless methods mentioned above, the stage is already set. The declared global pandemic means the implementation of the cashless global world could quickly transpire and bring with it the restrictions of who can buy or sell. Only those who accept the mark of the beast will be allowed to buy or sell.

The time cannot be long before the end of this world takes place. Jesus is coming back soon as He said He would. All the things He said would happen are happening now. The global pandemic is not even much of a surprise to anyone who has read and understood their Bible. Now is a good time to acquaint yourself with what others may tell you is foolishness without proof. The Bible can indeed be proven and a relationship with God is the only thing that can keep you sane and peaceful in a world that is going upside down.

Next we shall continue to unlock the 666 code and identify the mark of the beast so it may be clear when it comes and so that when it comes, choosing it becomes just that, a choice.

My personal advice is:

Keep away from the scary media and do not follow every minute of the bad state of the world. It will not do you any good but harm and fill you with anxiety. And this advice actually comes from Phillipians 4:8 which says "Finally, brethren, whatsoever things are true, whatsoever things are honest, whatsoever things are just, whatsoever things are pure, whatsoever things are lovely, whatsoever things are of good report; if there be any virtue, and if there be any praise, think on these things."

If the media is not bringing you a good report then you do not want to keep your mind on it at all but rather keep away from it! May God bless you and remove the fear of the future and that of the unknown today.

2 THE MARK OF GOD

Now there was a day when the sons of God came to present themselves before the LORD, and Satan came also among them. (Job 1:6)

In its simplest terms, a mark is a sign. If we want to understand anything about what the Bible teaches, then we must appreciate the counterfeiting creativity of Satan. For almost all things God has made, Satan has come up with his own inferior but well impressive version of a lookalike.

Satan not only has his cheap imitations in material objects. He is powerful and capable of creating spiritual fake things. He has at his disposal a third of the angels of God with whom he was kicked out of heaven. All these powerful agents are always working and ready to work with Satan against God's people. As such humans are never left alone by the evil one.

At the end of the literal week of creation, the Bible says that God rested on the seventh day. It calls this resting day the Sabbath. Many modern languages of the world still retain the word Sabbath in their vocabulary to refer to the seventh day. In Romanian, being just one example from a language I am familiar with, the seventh day of the week is called Sambata and when it is pronounced it clearly sounds like Sabbath.

Saturday is the seventh day of the week and therefore it is the Sabbath of God. But Satan the master counterfeiter has deceived many innocent millions of people that Sunday is the Sabbath. He has come up with some lies purporting to imply that Jesus authorised the disciples or the church to change the Sabbath day but Biblical evidence for this change does not exist. God wrote the Sabbath as a commandment that forms his law and His character. He wrote on a tablet of stone and He declared that He does not change.

The Sabbath is the mark of God which is a memorial of creation. The study and thorough and clear understanding of the original is critical for developing the ability to spot the fake. Therefore I would urge anybody learning about the true and original Sabbath to do their own diligent research about the Sabbath and who changed it and why. Study the Bible to find out what it says about who would seek to change times and laws of God.

When you have reached an understanding and when you have followed the history of the changes you will be ready to look into what the mark of the beast means.

May God fill you with wisdom today as you study His word.

3 THE MARK OF THE BEAST

There is a way which seemeth right unto a man, but the end thereof are the ways of death. (Proverbs 14:12)

After identifying the counterfeiting creativity and deceptive nature of Satan for everything God has made it is now time to identify Satan's mark.

This in no way suggests that any individual at this time has got this mark on themselves. It also does not disrespect any God loving person who has not reached the understanding of the meaning of the mark. Many millions of God loving people have no clue about what is going on and for them do I feel the burden to clarify this issue in a very simple way.

It is critical to note that by its very nature, deception can only succeed if it appears to be true and innocent. For deception to be convincing it needs to appear so real. There is no point for God to warn us so much about Satan's craftiness and cunningness if there is no danger paused by Satan.

Eve fell for the trap because she was promised good results and not evil ones. All it took was a miracle talking serpent and the introduction of the element of doubt in Eve's mind. She instantly missed the fact that Satan was effectively telling her in a twisted and hidden way that God was lying. Then she wanted the falsely promised result offered by Satan when he told her that she would not surely die. The very same lies Satan still tells people even today and they believe that they do not die.

The third of the angels cast out of heaven with Satan were super intelligent spirit beings who fell for what Lucifer presented as something good, being good but without God.

In the wilderness, as Jesus was weak from a 40 day fast, Satan came and gave his deceptive art the best shot. So if he could be so smart as to attempt to take on Jesus Himself, then how easy would it be to entice us with his lies?

The people living during Noah's time (known as the antediluvians) had never seen any rain before. The Bible describes them as people in whose hearts there was evil continually. They probably felt good in themselves and considered that God understood why they were how they were. For 120 years they were offered the chance to be saved and to come to God's way. But they chose the alternative offered by Satan. That alternative which seemed good enough to them but which was nothing but deceptive destruction.

The mark of God being his seventh day Sabbath has been replaced by Satan's craftiness in telling the church that it has the power to alter God's law. If it had not been so important then God would not have written it on stone and commanded the Israelites to remember the Sabbath day to keep it holy. The Mark of Satan therefore is Sunday sacredness which has no biblical backing. Everyone has the choice to either follow God or man.

At this point the mark of the beast has not been enforced on anyone yet by law. But the time is now very near for the people to be persuaded that the global woes are being caused by failing to honour God's day of rest. But note that the majority of people have no clue about which day of the week God's Sabbath is.

Dear reader, God is not happy for anyone to perish. The ark was available for more than just Noah and His family, but people had a choice. Even now God is not willing for any to perish. You are now informed about something you probably did not understand before. You cannot remain the same as before and say you are innocent. It is definitely still between you and your God but God is revealing things like this to you for your benefit. The Sabbath was made for you and you will never know the blessing of resting and worshipping your God on the day he commands you to until you experience it. May God bless you and guide you along into His truth and out of Satan's deception.

Shortly I will explain the number 666 and how it relates to Sunday as the mark of Satan's lordship. I will also touch on some aspects of why Sunday became the choice for many and how some people have been misled to think God agrees with their choice.

Please note that there is NO place in the Bible in which you will find the number 777. Yet there are many 7s that you will find in the Bible. So 777 as a number does not exist anywhere in the Scriptures

4 777 VERSUS 666

Here is wisdom. Let him that hath understanding count the number of the beast: for it is the number of a man; and his number is Six hundred threescore and six. (Revelation 13:18)

After noting that Satan is a deceiver it is fitting to point out some of his deceptions. We must never forget that Satan's powers were not removed from him when he was cast out of heaven. He has power to perform miracles. He can give people a lot of 'blessings' too and enable huge successes to happen for people in this world.

The many bad things that happen in this world are falsely charged against God. Even insurance companies accuse God for all the bad weather and natural disasters that happen. They call these phenomena 'acts of God'. But when we take a peek into how God functions we can relabel the disasters correctly as acts of Satan. We can see from the book of Job that God only permitted Satan to cause all the misery and disaster in Job's life. God was not the one who killed Job's children and Job' s animals. It was not God who put disease onto Job but Satan.

In the parable of the wheat and the tares, Jesus' response about who was responsible for the tares found where the wheat was planted was, “an enemy has done this”. Yet I can almost hear someone accusing God for not stopping Satan from doing all the evil he does.To this important point we shall come to in a little while but for now just understand that if God would not be intervening the bad situations we see could be a lot worse. But He does say in the same parable of tares and wheat that the tares and the wheat will be allowed to grow together and the tares will be dealt with later. In other words good and evil are being allowed but just for the present time only.

When the Egyptian magicians tried to counterfeit the miracles presented to Pharaoh by Aaron, their might fell shot of God’s as their serpents made by Satan’s power were swallowed by Aaron’s. Man’s power as given by Satan will never reach the power of God. God’s completeness throughout the Bible has repeatedly appeared in 7s. The creation week was a 7 day week. There are several other things like the 7 churches in Revelation and 7 trumpets and 7 plagues.

When one conceptualises the completeness of God against the fact that man's best could never reach God's, a numerical pattern of 777 for God can be placed against 666 for man. That is all the wisdom we need, to understand. There is nothing that requires trigonometric geniusness in computing complex numbers to decode some deep secret behind 666. Many variations and number manipulations have been computed to suit peoples purposes like saying the number meant Alexander the Great, the Catholic Pope or even Aldolf Hitler. It does not mean any of that but it simply means that when Satan has done his best to counterfeit God's work there will always be a lack of completeness to reach the 777 by God.

There is no need to fear the number 666 or to like the number 777. The digits have no spiritual significance or supernatural powers in them. Yet there is a need to make a choice about whose side we want to be on. I pray that we choose to be on the side of our creator and life giver. We need to revere the word of the one who has brought us out of the darkness and into His marvellous light. We are not at liberty to decide to trivialise the explicit commandments of God just because man says that they are not important anymore. Nobody has the right to say that God does not really mean what He says anymore than Satan had the right to tell Eve that God did not really mean what He said to Adam and Eve.

5 WHO CHANGED THE LAW OF GOD?

And he shall speak great words against the most High, and shall wear out the saints of the most High, and think to change times and laws: and they shall be given into his hand until a time and times and the dividing of time. (Daniel 7:25)

The fourth commandment says "Remember the Sabbath day to keep it holy". It continues to instruct that we should do all our work in six days and leave the Sabbath day free for worshipping and communing with God. The fact that it is given as a reminder to the Israelites indicates that the Sabbath preceded mount Sinai. The Sabbath indeed predated the Jews since its inception was at creation. Additionally the reminder serves to remind future generations who in time would forget the Sabbath.

The forgetting of the Sabbath had a mischievous catalytic involvement of the devil who always uses people. The change began centuries ago with anti-Judaism that started during the reign of Constantine the Great. Constantin was a Roman Emperor who ruled between AD 306 and 337[1].

Constantine made Sunday a public holiday and then made a law requiring all workers to rest on the venerable day of the sun. Many Christians ignored the edict until the church forbade observance of the Sabbath (Saturday) in the mid 360s.

---

[1] https://en.wikipedia.org/wiki/Constantine_the_Great

Since Constantine had been a sun worshipper before becoming a Christian, he made Christianity the empire's state religion. But he mixed his sun worship tradition with Christian beliefs. He changed the day of worship from Sabbath to Sunday but it was the Council of Laodecia of AD 363-364 which forbade Christians from observing the Biblical Sabbath. The Romans had misrepresented the observance of the Sabbath and jubilee Sabbath year as laziness. So the Sabbath became increasingly unpopular following this misrepresentation.

The same Laodecian council changed the Biblical name for the Sabbath to the pagan name Saturday in honour of Saturn the pagan deity. The Roman state transferred the day of worship to Sunday in honour of sun worship and to make a distinct difference from the Jews. They called Sabbath keeping Judaising and declared that Judaising was now illegal. Christians now had to prove that they had revoked their original God appointed Sabbath by working on Sabbath.

The change thus carried out officially by the church and state helped in the forgetting of God's Sabbath day. Boastingly the changers even use the word 'mark' to signify that the change was their mark rather than God's mark.

There are plenty of quotes with the said boastfulness but I will pick just a couple as examples.

"Of course the Catholic Church claims that the change [of the Sabbath to Sunday] was her act . . AND THE ACT IS A MARK of her ecclesiastical power."—From the office of Cardinal Gibbons, through Chancellor H. F. Thomas, November 11, 1895[2]

"Sunday is a Catholic institution, and its claim to observance can be defended only on Catholic principles . . From beginning to end of Scripture there is not a single passage that warrants the transfer of weekly public worship from the last day of the week to the first."—Catholic Press, Sydney, Australia, August, 1900.[3]

I would urge anyone who doubts any of these things to do their own diligent research. Any keen reader who wants to establish facts can do so in seconds.

The truth about the mark of God and the mark of the beast now stands clear before you. History is all the proof you need to authenticate the reliability and accuracy of the Bible. But before reaching out to the future I would like to demonstrate further, that the Bible can be trusted to reveal what is just unfolding now before our very own eyes. The next few pages should highlight the Bible's accuracy.

---

[2] https://www.seventh-day.org/historians.htm

[3] Ibid

6 STANDING NEXT TO THE CYRUS CYLINDER

Now in the first year of Cyrus king of Persia, that the word of the LORD by the mouth of Jeremiah might be fulfilled, the LORD stirred up the spirit of Cyrus king of Persia, that he made a proclamation throughout all his kingdom, and put it also in writing, saying, Thus saith Cyrus king of Persia, The LORD God of heaven hath given me all the kingdoms of the earth; and he hath charged me to build him an house at Jerusalem, which is in Judah.
Who is there among you of all his people? his God be with him, and let him go up to Jerusalem, which is in Judah, and build the house of the LORD God of Israel, (he is the God,) which is in Jerusalem. (Ezra 1:1-3)

At the end of the year 2018 I had the privilege of touring the British Museum in London as part of a group. I had the chance to see a number of things that can only be found in the British Museum. These are items which have been found by archeologists and preserved by curators because of their historical significance. From these archeological historical artefacts can be found some remarkable proofs of the accuracy of the Biblical text.

One specific item of historical significance that I was absolutely thrilled by and that I even took a photograph of myself standing next to is called the Cyrus Cylinder. The Cyrus Cylinder can be found exhibited in Room 55 of the British Museum in London. It is an ancient clay cylinder on which some writing is inscribed.

Before stating the content of the text on the cylinder I mention a couple of things of prophetic importance. Jeremiah 25:11-12 which was written around 626 to 586 BC predicts that the Jewish people would be enslaved by the Babylonians for 70 years. Secondly, Isaiah 13:17 which was written between 701 and 681 BC predicts that the Medes would attack Babylon.

According to the inscription on the cylinder, Cyrus released the Jews and allowed them to return to Jerusalem in the year 539 BC after being Babylonian slaves from 609 BC. Thus the 70 year prophecy was fulfilled to the letter as was that of the Medes attacking Babylon which happened in 639 BC. What is even more fascinating is that 150 years before he was even born the book of Isaiah 45:1 had Cyrus' name and role in allowing the Jews to rebuild the temple in Jerusalem prophesied.

Later in the book we shall return to Cyrus but for now let us look at the inscription on the Cylinder. Part of the text on the Cyrus Cylinder as translated into modern English reads:

"I am Cyrus, king of the universe, the great king, the powerful king, king of Babylon, king of Sumer and Akkad, king of the four quarters of the world, son of Cambyses, the great king, king of the city of Anshan, grandson of Cyrus, the great king, ki[ng of the ci]ty of Anshan, descendant of Teispes, the great king, king of the city of Anshan, the perpetual seed of kingship, whose reign Bel (Marduk) and Nabu love, and with whose kingship, to their joy, they concern themselves. When I went as harbinger of peace into Babylon I founded my sovereign residence within the palace amid celebration and rejoicing."[4]

The Cyrus Cylinder which is an archaeological artefact, though some people may not like it, proves the accuracy of the Bible. Yet it is only just one thing among many other historical objects that inadvertently corroborate the Biblical text. Later the importance of Cyrus in the unfolding of current and last day events shall become apparent. May God bless you.

[4] https://www.ancient.eu/article/166/the-cyrus-cylinder/ accessed 30 March 2020
by **Antoine Simonin** published on 18 January 2012

7 KING JEHU BOWS DOWN

But Jehu took no heed to walk in the law of the LORD God of Israel with all his heart: for he departed not from the sins of Jeroboam, which made Israel to sin. (2 Kings 10:31)

While I was enjoying my trip of discovery at the British Museum in London, the best part of my adventure was seeing the Bible coming to life. Indeed there are some things that can only be better appreciated when they are seen. For such profound and unique experiences one must indeed agree with the commonly used expression that says that a picture is worth a thousand words.

King Ahab is recorded in the Bible as a very evil king. When Ahab died, the prophet Elisha according to the book of 2 Kings 9 &10, instructed Jehu the military commander of the chariots of Israel to exterminate king Ahab's entire family and become the king himself. Jehu did as the prophet had ordered killing Jezebel, Ahab's queen and Ahab's entire dynasty with 70 sons. Jehu also cleaned up Israel of all the legacy of evil left by king Ahab including Baal worship and Baal worshippers .

After obliterating Ahab's family, Jehu reigned over the northern kingdom of Israel for 28 years until the year 814 BC. But in his first year as the king he wanted the protection of king Shalmeneser III of Assyria against Hazael of Damascus, a common enemy. So he attempted to buy the allegiance of Shalmeneser III by paying him homage, something that no other king of Israel had ever done before.

The act of Jehu paying homage and bowing down to the Assyrian king seems to not only have caused a stir in those ancient days but to have warranted being engraved onto a rock.The black obelisk in the British Museum in London depicts Jehu bowing down in homage to Shalmeneser III. The cuneiform inscription on the obelisk states that the man bowing down in homage is Jehu. The translated text of the Assyrian cuneiform inscription reads, "The tribute of Jehu, son of Omri: I received from him silver, gold, a golden bowl, a golden vase with pointed bottom, golden tumblers, golden buckets, tin, a staff for a king [and] spears."

The Bible only states that Jehu did not follow the law of the Lord. The details of just how low he went and even put Israel to shame by dependence on Shalmeneser III instead of God is revealed by the obelisk. Yet the same obelisk serves to confirm that there indeed was a king called Jehu as the Bible states.

Historians and archaeologists as well as museum curators have provided evidence that complements the Bible. Discovering these kinds of things is nothing but a thrill. I was delighted to have had the opportunity to see another piece of historical evidence to prove the accuracy of the Bible. Be filled with peace today that you can trust the Bible.

8 SHALMENESER III, BRAGGING KING OF ASSYRIA

And they continued three years without war between Syria and Israel. (1 Kings 22:1)

Come with me today if you will, into the British Museum in London, England. Let us enter through the museum doors and then go straight into room number 6A. There we find a 2.2metre tall limestone monolith (stela), a very important artefact that was dug up in the year 1861 in Turkey. There is nowhere we can miss it as it stands prominently and tall against the wall. This stela is here to show Assyrian history for the period between the 9th and 7th century BC. But it gives us an insight of some details that are not recorded in the Bible but yet show that the Bible is true and accurate.

The stela is inscribed with rather gory details of the battles fought by Shalmeneser III (859-824 BC). These records are important because it was Shalmeneser III who attacked Phoenicia (modern Palestine) during the reign of king Ahab of Israel according to 1 Kings 22.

Though we cannot decipher or understand any of the cuneiform inscriptions, we find translated into English, at the end of the monolith a description of the battle of Qarqar, the Syrian city. In this battle is a coalition of 12 kings led by king Hadadezer of Damascus and king Irhuleni of Hamath plus also a large force led by king Ahab of Israel. The coalition is formed at the request of king Irhuleni who wants to stave off Assyrian aggression by Shalmeneser III.

Showing the exact whereabouts of king Ahab, the monolith inscription of the battle at Qarqar provides us with a date 853 BC and effectively an answer to the mystery paused by 1 Kings 22.1 about the truce. It also confirms that king Ahab had a large army. The translation of some of the text on the monolith reads:

> "I destroyed, devastated, and set fire to Karkar, his royal city. <Irhulêni> brought twelve kings to his support; they came against me to offer battle and fight: 1,200 chariots, 1,200 cavalry, and 20,000 soldiers belonging to Hadad-ezer of Damascus; 700 chariots, 700 cavalry, and 10,000 [or 20,000] soldiers belonging to Irhuleni of Hama; 2,000 chariots, and 10,000 soldiers belonging to Ahab, the Israelite[A-ha-ab-bu Sir-ila-a-a];"

The Bible has no explanation of why king Ahab and king Benhadad of Damascus ceased their hostilities for 3 years. The monolith inscription therefore helps clear the mystery. There is an obvious exaggeration on the inscription implying a bloodbath of the coalition but not backed up by the taking of land. Many artefacts in the museum bear such braggings by various kings. So it may be more accurate to say that the battle of Qarqar was not won by Shalmeneser but rather it was stopped by the coalition.

The delight of seeing ancient historical archaeology bringing out some bits that are not stated in the Bible is simply just phenomenal. It is good to see historical evidence that is in support of the Bible and with great precision at that.

May my experience of museum proofs reassure you that when you are reading the Bible you are reading a book inspired by God to be written by humans. May many blessings be yours today.

9 TABLETS OF CLAY

And all the people saw the thunderings, and the lightnings, and the noise of the trumpet, and the mountain smoking: and when the people saw it, they removed, and stood afar off.
And they said unto Moses, Speak thou with us, and we will hear: but let not God speak with us, lest we die. (Exodus 20:18-19)

When Moses came back down from mount Sinai, according to Exodus 34, his face shone brightly and in his hands he carried the eternal law of God written with God's own finger on two tablets of stone. What an incredible story, except that it is not just a story but it is reality and not fictional. This was precisely how the Ten Commandments were given by God to mankind. The Israelites were the first to receive them but they apply to all humans. If you are not familiar with them then you may want to turn to the book of Exodus 20 in the Bible for a few minutes and have a read. May you experience a blessing from God as you read His word and encounter His law.

The ancient practice of writing on stone tablets has preserved many writings that have been uncovered in excavations by archaeologists and placed in the British Museum for all to see living history. Even those who may choose to say that they do not believe in the Bible have to admit that some of the things unearthed by archaeologists and that are not even in the Bible confirm what is in the Bible to be true. For those of us who already have the blessed experience of trusting the Bible, discovering the additional writings found underground and preserved for centuries fills us with awe and thrill. Such was my experience on the day I found out of the existence of stone tablets full of writings and curated by expert historians and artefacts scientists.

Before delving into some other contents of the Bible which will lead us steadily towards our present day events, I want to highlight a bit more of the historical aspects brought out in archaeological findings. Remaining within the confines of the British Museum in London, we look at the clay tablets upstairs. Thousands upon thousands of tablets exist which tell a lot of stories from the ancient world. Our interest is captivated by the existence of tablets that came from the Euphrates, Mesopotamia, Syria and Egypt. From these we find inscriptions that talk of and confirm the Biblical account of the existence of the cities of Sodom and Gomorrah. We also get a confirmation of the name Ur where the Bible states that Abraham came from but has nothing written about in history. Finally we are interested in the tablets that give credibility to the creation and the flood about which the Bible speaks.

On one particular clay tablet, there is what is referred to as the Gilgamesh Epic, an epic poem from ancient Mesopotamia. Gilgamesh was the king of Uruk from around 2100BC[5]. From this tablet is believed to have been the source of the book of Genesis in the Bible. Reading the translated story though shows it full of things that are not exactly what

---

[5] https://en.wikipedia.org/wiki/Epic_of_Gilgamesh

appears to be Biblical material. Nonetheless the core of the story does parallel what is found in the Bible. These tablets predate the writing of the Bible.

Part of the translation of the Gilgamesh Epic reads, "Life, which you look for, you will never find. For when the gods created man, they let death be his share, and life withheld in their own hands".

There are over 200 different ancient cultures who tell the story of the flood which proves the universal acceptability of the deluge's occurrence. The Bible account is the only one written in a way that clearly elaborates the beginnings of life. What the tablets do is to help show that even before the Bible existed as we know it, God was known to the people of old. The book of Genesis is the basis from which all the other books of the Bible are written.

As you go through your day today may you be blessed to know that God has given us His word through the Bible and preserved it through thousands of years. May you cherish The Bible.

10 A QUICK PEEK OF THE SANCTUARY

There are priests that offer gifts according to the law: Who serve unto the example and shadow of heavenly things, as Moses was admonished of God when he was about to make the tabernacle: for, See, saith he, that thou make all things according to the pattern shewed to thee in the mount. (Hebrews 8:4-5)

In the Bible, the sanctuary was the dwelling place of God. He instructed Moses and said let them make me a sanctuary that I may dwell among them (Exodus 25:8). God provided the exact details, including measurements, for how the sanctuary was meant to be made. The entire sanctuary with its structure and function had symbolic meanings. In this section, I will give just a quick overview of the meanings before going deeper into other profound aspects about the sanctuary that can be imaginatively traced throughout scripture.

The first item in the courtyard of the sanctuary was the altar of sacrifice where the animals were sacrificed. It symbolised the sacrifice of Jesus dying on the cross for our sins (Hebrews 10:10) when He was sinless.

The laver was used for the washing of hands and feet by the priest before ministering in the holy sanctuary. The laver symbolised baptism (Mark 1:4) which in itself is a symbol of dying to sin and being buried in the watery grave then resurrecting into life as a new and changed creation.

The table of shewbread had 12 loaves of bread that was eaten only by the priests. The bread symbolised the word of God as the Bible says man shall not live by bread alone but by every word that proceedeth out of the mouth of God (Matthew 4:4).

The altar of incense was where incense was burned every morning and evening. This symbolised the prayers of the people ascending constantly to God as the smoke from the incense was constantly rising.

The 7 branch candlestick provided light. It symbolised the light of Jesus who says I am the light of the world (John 8:12). Jesus also said His followers are also light as He told them "You are the light of the world, a city on a hill cannot be hid and neither do men light a candle and put it under a bushel" (Matthew 5:14-16)

The ark of the covenant was located in the most holy place of the sanctuary also referred to as the holy of holies. On the ark was the mercy seat between two cherubims (angels) who symbolically guarded the ark. Inside the ark were the ten commandments. The covenant was that if the children of Israel kept the 10 commandments as they were given to Moses then God would always be in their presence.

The sanctuary is one profound element found in the Bible that deserves to be studied and well understood. Dare I say, the more one gets a clearer understanding of the meaning of the sanctuary, the clearer the rest of the Bible becomes? In the next few chapters I shall endeavour to bring out more profound lessons on the sanctuary. May God bless you and make you yearn for His word which gives life eternal.

11 SATAN REBELS AGAINST THE SANCTUARY AND PULLS US ALONG

Thy way, O God, is in the sanctuary: who is so great a God as our God? (Psalm 77:13)

Before he became Satan, Lucifer was an angel who was responsible for defending and protecting the law of God in heaven. He is described as a covering cherub in Ezekiel 28:14. In verse 15 he is said to have been perfect from the day he was created until iniquity was found in him. He had now turned against the very law of God whose job was his to cover and defend. So the very first war that was ever fought was over the law of God (Isaiah 14:12), the ten commandments.

A commonly asked question is just how did Lucifer manage to deceive a third of the angels of heaven? Lucifer actually wanted to be good; to ascend and be like God, to be righteous and holy like God. So Lucifer appealed to them by saying that they could be holy like God, without the law of God. This was the beginning of what exists even now as self righteousness.

Again, a question is asked, why did God not just destroy Satan and hence eliminate all evil at that time once and for all? Deuteronomy 19:16-19 lays out a principle given to Moses and the children of Israel. The principle was that whenever a controversy arose there had to be a third party to judge. The same principle of third party judgement was what God was going to use. But at that time, only God and the angels and only Lucifer and his team of angels existed. So making any judgement at that point would have seemed unjust.

So Satan and his angels, a third of the angels of heaven were cast out. God wants to give Satan and his angels a fair trial. He wants to allow a third party who has no knowledge of the crime and who was not even at the scene to judge. That third party who will judge the angels is us, created human beings (1 Corinthians 6:3) who were not even there when the problem occurred.

As Satan watches the events unfolding at the time of creation, he sees that these creations are the ones who will judge him. Then he hashes a plan to bribe the judges. He goes to Eve, covertly calling God a liar and tells her that she can be just like God (exactly what he said to the angels) and a good judge if only she eats the fruit (Genesis 3:4-5). Eve and Adam both fall into Satan's trap and they are immediately disqualified from being judges and thrown out of the garden of Eden. But Jesus comes and gives a promise to restore them to their original condition of knowing right from wrong and become law abiding citizens again. The sanctuary has the purpose to help people to become law abiding citizens and honour all of God's commandments.

Next we shall creatively trace just how the sanctuary permeates all through the gospel message and why we should understand it. I pray that today you may appreciate the plan of salvation that Jesus came to die to redeem us from sin when Satan trapped us and offered us false happiness.

12 TRACING SANCTUARY SYMBOLISMS THROUGH ISRAEL

And their charge shall be the ark, and the table, and the candlestick, and the altars, and the vessels of the sanctuary wherewith they minister, and the hanging, and all the service thereof. (Numbers 3:31)

As we are familiar with the meaning of the symbols in the sanctuary we can now search the Bible stories and try to see if we can discover some things fitting into the meaning. Come with me through the exodus of the Israelites from Egypt and let us attempt to discover the sanctuary.

As God is about to call the Israelites out of captivity He gives them a sanctuary, which really is something special and has God’s way. Psalm 77:13 says “Thy way O God is in the sanctuary” so when God gives Israel the sanctuary He gives them His way. Lucifer rebelled against God because he did not like God's way.

When God is getting ready to use Israel to bring salvation to the world, He gives them a replica of what was already in heaven to take the way of salvation to the world. Jesus Himself says that He is the way, the truth and the life. For three thousand years before Jesus came, the sanctuary’s existence symbolically prophesied that he would come and die on the cross for our sins.

For better comprehension, I highly recommend a deeper study of the sanctuary directly from the Bible itself.

Just before Israel is delivered from Egypt, God tells the people to make a sacrifice and put the blood on the doorposts (Exodus 12). This brings to my mind the symbol of the altar of sacrifice from the sanctuary services.

After the death of his first son, Pharaoh finally lets the children of Israel go. They travel for a while before they come to a dead end. Right in front of them is the red sea when they are meant to be on the other side of it. Behind them they observe, with terror, that Pharaoh and his army are hurriedly pursuing them. Pharaoh has changed his mind about letting them go after all and he wants them back to serve him and work for him. He cannot stand to lose his free labourers, his slaves.

God performs a profound miracle right at that moment. The red sea opens up and forms a wall of water on either side to allow the children of Israel to cross on dry ground. But just as they get to the other end of the path through the seabed, Pharaoh's army rides their chariots into the same riverbed path. Then God lets the sea go back into its place again and the water reunites while swallowing up the army and the pharaoh. With some imagination I say this allows the symbol of baptism by immersion to take place for Pharaoh and his army. If you permit this creative imagination then you will see the laver in the sanctuary structure symbolised here. (Exodus 14)

Back in comfort and safety as Pharaoh and his troops have been drowned, the Israelites journey on. They forget the miracle they have just seen as they get hungry. They start telling Moses that they should rather have remained in Egypt and eaten the garlic and fish and leeks and melons of Egypt. Questioning him about why he brought them out to die in the desert as if there were no graves in Egypt, they tell him that they would have preferred to die in Egypt than out in the desert. Then God miraculously rains manna for them from heaven. Putting this into sanctuary symbolism would fit squarely as the table of shewbread (Exodus 16).

In Exodus 19 God says to Israel, "You are a peculiar people, my light to the world". This reminds us of the 7 candlesticks in sanctuary symbolisms. God says to them, "I want you to take my message to the world". In the same chapter He also tells them to spend 3 days preparing themselves and praying. This heart preparation reminds us of the altar of incense in the sanctuary. They are to prepare because in Exodus 20 God gives them the 10 commandments which, in the sanctuary, are found in the ark of the covenant.

The pattern of the sanctuary given here is an extremely creative one. Yet this hopefully makes a point that there is a lot one can discover in the Bible. There can be some fun in reading the Bible and noticing some patterns that are hidden in plain sight. I hope you are motivated to dig for yourself some things out of the Bible that are not so obvious. May God bless you as you ponder over the way of God.

13 THE LIFE OF CHRIST AND THE SANCTUARY

Thy word is a lamp unto my feet, and a light unto my path. (Psalm 119:105)

In continuing to search for patterns of the sanctuary in the Scriptures we find the life of Christ fitting neatly into the pattern. As we walk into the sanctuary from the courtyard where we first encounter the altar of sacrifice we recall where Jesus's birth took place. Jesus was born in Bethlehem when Mary and Joseph were travelling for a population census that had been decreed by Caesar Augustus.

There was no room for them at the hotels or inns of the time for them to spend the night. Everywhere they tried they were being told that the places were fully booked. Finally they got to somewhere where the owner of the place offered them a very humble alternative to stay in. This alternative was a stable. It so happened that during the night, Jesus Christ the Saviour of mankind who owns everything, was born in a manger and among the animals. Thinking of this, along the sanctuary subject, we can say that Jesus the lamb of God, was fittingly born where animals belong or on an altar of sacrifice.

In His life, Jesus did many things. He taught in

the synagogue and He helped in His father's carpentry work. When He reached the age of 30, His cousin, John the baptist saw Him coming towards him to be baptised and proclaimed, "Behold the Lamb of God, which taketh away the sin of the world."(John 1:29). The baptism of Jesus when thought of in terms of the sanctuary symbolised the laver.

More accurately though, the laver symbolised the baptism rather than the other way round.

After His baptism, Jesus was led into the wilderness to be tempted by Satan. He was very hungry after fasting for forty days and forty nights. The very first temptation that was made on Him was being asked to turn stones into bread. Bread in the sanctuary was found on the table of shewbread. So we have a match.

The second temptation of Jesus was for Him to be asked to throw Himself down from the cliff and offer a presumptuous prayer to God. This matches the altar of incense in the sanctuary. Satan was trying to counterfeit God's way which he knew too well.

The third temptation on Jesus was being taken onto a high mountain and being shown all the kingdoms of the world, His people, His 7 candlesticks in the sanctuary. He was then asked to bow down and worship the devil before the devil could give Him His people.

Jesus overcame all the temptations and went on to preach the law combined with the mercy of God. The law of God was found in the ark of the covenant in the most holy place of the sanctuary.

Looking at the same life of Christ from the other direction of the sanctuary outwards we can say that Jesus left His throne of holiness in the heavenly sanctuary. He lived a life of prayer, on the altar of incense. He also lived a life based on the word of God, the table of shewbread. He let His light shine, the 7 candlesticks before He was baptised (the laver) and then crucified or sacrificed on the altar of sacrifice.

A lot of imagination has been employed again in this attempt to find a sanctuary pattern through the life of Christ. If you search hard enough you can find it throughout the Bible. May you be blessed as you look for interesting patterns in the Bible.

14 REMOVAL OF THE SANCTUARY FROM ISRAEL

Esaias also crieth concerning Israel, Though the number of the children of Israel be as the sand of the sea, a remnant shall be saved: For he will finish the work, and cut it short in righteousness: because a short work will the Lord make upon the earth. (Romans 9:27-28)

The Bible's Old Testament widely shows how the devil tries to destroy the sanctuary's importance, and also how he attacks the people who have the sanctuary. He hates the sanctuary and its significance so he targets anyone who tries to follow God's way.

Israel having been given the sanctuary by God should understand His ways, but they succumb to bad behaviour and rebellion. Because Israel is so rebellious God ultimately allows them to fall into Babylonian captivity.

To the Israelites is given a prophecy (70 weeks) saying if they do not not receive Jesus, the one who the sanctuary points to, who is coming in 70 weeks, and if they continue to rebel, God will take away the sanctuary and I will give it to others (Daniel 9:25).

Jesus comes, according to the prophecy, Israel rejects Christ and the veil in the temple is ripped in two from top to bottom signifying the end of the earthly sacrifices (Mark 15:35).

After His resurrection, Jesus goes to heaven to the heavenly sanctuary and the earthly sanctuary is taken from literal Israel and given to what can be termed spiritual Israel (Galatians 3:28 says there is no longer Jew or Gentile) which is all who accept Christ.

God gives Israel the gift of tongues to spread the message of the heavenly sanctuary and heavenly high priest everywhere (Acts 2:4-19). The devil is angry and he raises literal Israel to attack spiritual Israel. (Acts 13:50) Then literal Rome to attack spiritual Israel. But he realises that every time a Christian dies the seed of christianity multiplies exponentially. (Acts 7-14)

God's way is hated by Satan and He stirs up people to destroy it. But it shall endure forever and multiply continually until the whole world hears about it. Read your Bible to find God's peace in times of turmoil. May you have the peace and joy of God's love.

15 SATAN MAKES COUNTERFEITS OF SANCTUARY MEANINGS

For by grace are ye saved through faith; and that not of yourselves: it is the gift of God. (Ephesians 2:8)

After realising that the gospel was expanding exponentially with each Christian martyr, Satan decided to employ new strategies.

Using the very institution that should have been supporting and promoting the unadulterated word of God Satan caused the priests to prevent anyone except the ordained priests from teaching God's word. This ushered in the period that became known as the dark ages. The people had to rely upon the priest to decide what was true and what they needed to know. The people had no access to reading the Bible for themselves. By depriving the people of the word of God, Satan had successfully taken a shot at the table of shewbread.

The church taught that traditions were more important than the word of God and then they created a two compartment room divided by a curtain (similar to the veil in the sanctuary separating the holy from the most holy place) and got a man to sit behind the curtain in place of God to hear the confessions of another human being. They also introduced the sacrament of penance where they collected money (called indulgences) for the purported forgiveness of sins when God gives his grace and salvation free of charge.

While at it they took down the ten commandments and modified them to replace God's seventh day Sabbath with the first day of the week as a day of worship and rest.

One other thing Satan attacked was the laver. The church introduced an alternative to the baptism of John the baptist. While the very word baptism is taken from a Greek word baptizo meaning immersion, the church brought in sprinkling as a new method of baptism. Not only did they bring sprinkling but they also started baptising infants. The Bible says one who believes and repents from their sins should be baptised. Infant baptism cannot be because of believing and repenting. So Satan really hates baptism enough to distort it this way.

The attack on the sanctuary by Satan has been ongoing for centuries. Yet as we read the end of the Holy Bible we have the assurance that in the end it is God who prevails over Satan. But in the meantime we need to move closer to God and further away from Satan. Prayerfully studying the Bible for yourself helps in transforming the character and is helpful in learning more about God.

16 WYCLIFFE AND THE GRADUAL RESTORATION OF THE SANCTUARY

And he said unto me, Unto two thousand and three hundred days; then shall the sanctuary be cleansed. (Daniel 8:14)

The restoration and cleansing of the sanctuary took place over a period of about 5 centuries. Starting with John Wycliffe, one brave English theologian thought to be born in the 1320s the status quo of the day met with challenges. Alongside the work of Wycliffe was a thorn in the flesh for the church with two rival popes at the same time and a third one joining the rivalry later from 1409 until 1414.

John Wycliffe, who was from the county of Yorkshire, England was an ordained priest who had studied at the University of Oxford. He questioned the self-serving teachings of popes and clerics and declared that the scriptures were the only reliable guide to the truth about God. He attacked the selling of indulgences, the practice of praying to saints and he also argued that there was no scriptural justification for the existence of the papacy. He even said that the ruling of England should have no papal interference as England's monarchs and lay administrators only should rule England directly under Christ, not popes.

Pope Gregory VII condemned Wycliffe's views in 1377[6] but this did not deter the priest. Wycliffe's belief that Christians should learn the Scripture for themselves resulted in him translating the Bible into the language of the common people. In 1382 the first completed English translation of the Bible was issued, bringing the light of the Scripture back to the people and thus restoring the table of shewbread from the sanctuary.

Satan however did not relent in his attacks. In his lifetime, five different papal bills were issued for Wycliffe's arrest but yet he was never convicted as a heretic.[7] He died of a stroke on December 31 in 1384 and only in 1415 was he condemned posthumously as a heretic. They exhumed his body and burned it in 1428. Then they threw his ashes into the Swift river. But that did not eliminate the word of God from being spread to the world.

The chronicler Fuller later observed: "They burnt his bones to ashes and cast them into the Swift, a neighbouring brook running hard by. Thus the brook

---

6 https://www.historytoday.com/archive/john-wycliffe-condemned-heretic

7 http://strands.blogs.efca.org/2017/02/19/pre-reformation-john-wycliffe/

hath conveyed his ashes into Avon; Avon into Severn; Severn into the narrow seas; and they into the main ocean. And thus the ashes of Wycliffe are the emblem of his doctrine which now is dispersed the world over."[8]

Clearly, God used Wycliffe to enable the Bible to reach everyone. The trouble the word of God has been through should make us all cherish the treasure that it is. If only we would read the Bible we would discover the precious gems buried within its pages that could not be eliminated by Satan.

---

8 http://strands.blogs.efca.org/2017/02/19/pre-reformation-john-wycliffe/

17 LUTHER AND THE RESTORATION OF THE SANCTUARY

My little children, these things write I unto you, that ye sin not. And if any man sin, we have an advocate with the Father, Jesus Christ the righteous: And he is the propitiation for our sins: and not for ours only, but also for the sins of the whole world. (1 John 2:1-2)

Martin Luther was born on November 10, 1483, in Eisleben, Saxony, Germany. In 1507 he became a monk and a Catholic priest. Luther also became a professor of moral theology at Germany's University of Wittenberg. He translated the Bible into German for all his people to read God's Word for themselves. Luther thus played a role in restoring the table of shewbread in the sanctuary.

In his priestly role he witnessed the unjust ways of the church in taking money from the members and purporting to buy salvation from God. The teachings of the church made the people to fear hell fire and to despair about their loved ones who had died and were, according to the teachings, in purgatory. People were living with terror for their own death as they were convinced by the church that they were such wretched sinners and hence they lived with a torment of guilt. Driven by this fear and dread of burning in hell, the people felt obliged to buy indulgences (permits) from church to reduce the suffering after death.

The dignitaries of the church preached about living a life of humility and modesty while they themselves were living luxurious livelihoods. This was something everyone could feel but that nobody was speaking out against until Martin Luther did. In 1517 he wrote his famous ninety-five theses to start a debate about a list of things that the church practised. He nailed his theses on the door of the Castle Church in Wittenberg, Germany. He too had been tormented by how one could obtain God's mercy with money. His main arguments in the theses were that the church's selling of indulgences was unBiblical. This was the start of the protestant reformation. Luther argued that every Christian could speak directly to God and be answered and hence there was no need for the mediation via the priesthood of nuns and monks between God and man. He maintained that the Bible alone was the source of divine knowledge. Pope Leo X in 1520 and the Holy Roman Emperor Charles V at the Diet of Worms in 1521 demanded that Luther recant his writings (which by then were many). Luther refused to recant and was excommunicated by the pope and condemned as an outlaw.

In arguing that Christ's sacrifice and not penance pays for our sins Luther also helped restore the altar of sacrifice in the sanctuary which Satan had usurped. If we were living in Luther's time I would most probably have also been a Lutheran. I would read the Bible for myself even now as I would encourage you to read it too. May God bless you as you read the Holy Bible which helps liberate our minds from sin.

18 ZWINGLI RESTORATION OF THE SANCTUARY

And fear not them which kill the body, but are not able to kill the soul: but rather fear him which is able to destroy both soul and body in hell. (Matthew 10:28)

Ulrich Zwingli was born in Switzerland. There he grew up from a humble home and turned into an advocate for Biblical truth. He was opposed to the sacrament of transubstantiation which the church practised. They said that the communion bread and wine miraculously got transformed into the real body and real blood of Christ during communion (Eucharist). Zwingli rightly argued that the bread and wine were only symbols and the communion service was a memorial of Christ.
(Luke 22:19)

Although not in any discussion or communication with Martin Luther, Zwingli was also opposed to the payment of indulgences for penance. He said that the sacrifice of Christ was enough to pay for our sins. This is what the Bible teaches and so I say it has to be God who was directing both reformers who were far from each other.

Zwingli argued that statues and images that filled the places of worship were inappropriate and against the word of God. So he got them removed from the places of worship in Zurich. He enjoyed popular support for his teachings as he always referred his arguments to Scripture.

Another practise that Zwingli did not support was the practice of infant baptism and sprinkling of water as baptism. So he reintroduced the practice of baptism by immersion as it is in the Bible. Thus restoring the laver in the sanctuary.

The Swiss reformation happened completely independent from the German reformation. A lot of people joined in with the understanding of both Zwingli and Luther and started protests against Rome and in support of the reforms. That is how the protestant churches began, as people protested against Rome.

The Bible has such precious teachings that people like Zwingli literally sacrificed their very lives for (he died in Switzerland in a battle of protestants against Catholics). His last words when the soldiers killed him in battle were 'You can kill my body but you cannot kill my soul.'

It is therefore a good thing for us to become acquainted with the contents of the Bible. May you be blessed as you read.

19 CALVIN AND THE RESTORATION OF THE SANCTUARY

Seeing then that we have a great high priest, that is passed into the heavens, Jesus the Son of God, let us hold fast our profession. (Hebrews 4:14)

One of the most significant figures in Christian history, John Calvin, was born in the Picardy area of France in 1509. He grew into becoming a very prominent man in the reformation movement and in church history.

At as young an age as 14 he went left home for Paris to study and obtained a law degree from the University of Paris. As a devout Catholic, his father had originally wanted him to become a priest.

During Calvin's time as a student the move to protest against the teachings of the church was gathering momentum and he became involved. He continued with this involvement beyond his student days and so became an activist. He was so involved that his involvement made France an unsafe place for his radical reformation views.

Calvin moved to Switzerland where he published his first book, "The Institutes of the Christian Religion". Later He wrote commentaries on many books of the Bible. He espoused some dogmatic godliness that attracted many protestants who, for following him, became mockingly known as Calvinists. He was very strictly and totally against immorality, drunkenness, swearing, gambling and dancing.

Calvin also argued that Christ only and not the pope was the head of the church. As such there was only one universal church and so to become a body of Christ with Christ as the head, reformers had to leave the Roman Catholic church. Thus in the 1500s John Calvin, by showing from Scripture that people could directly go to God for themselves and not pray through priests, effectively restored the altar of incense in the sanctuary.

Calvin also maintained that nature or people could never reveal the will of God to mankind as could be done by the Bible and only the Bible. If I had lived during Calvin's time and learned of his arguments then I would most probably have also become a Calvinist. Yet I am thankful to have the opportunity of examining the Bible for myself as Calvin taught that all should do. May you be inspired and motivated to do the same for yourself too. May you experience God's blessings as you study His Bible.

20 SMYTH AND THE RESTORATION OF THE SANCTUARY

John did baptize in the wilderness, and preach the baptism of repentance for the remission of sins. (Mark 1:4)

In the year 1554, John Smyth was born in Sturton-le-Steeple, Nottinghamshire, England. He studied at Christ's College in Cambridge to become an Anglican priest. By his time the reformation movement seemed to have settled down following the death of Martin Luther and the setting up of the Counter-Reformation movement by the Council of Trent to convince or persuade protestants to return to the Catholic church.

Smyth found the teachings of his own Church of England as well as that of Zwingli, Luther and the Catholics to be incompatible with his understanding of the Scriptures.

Smyth thus left the Anglican church and then, under the threat of king James I who wanted everyone to conform by force, Smyth exiled to Amsterdam. Even in Amsterdam Smyth continued his defence of Bible truth. He wanted a church with no hierarchy but as in the book of Acts a church with only bishops and deacons who themselves were subject to lay people as exemplified by the Bible.

Condemning all established churches of his day as false, Smyth cited their methods of baptism and infant baptism practices as unbiblical. He rightly argued that only believing adults were baptised in the Bible.

He said that baptism consisted of three elements, namely: the baptism of the spirit, the confession of the mouth and then the washing with water. He questioned how anyone could just wash with water, in what he said was the least and last of baptism except those of great folly.

Smythe was fully convinced that he could not anywhere be baptised correctly in the biblical manner as that of John the Baptist. So he baptised himself before baptising 36 others who believed his teachings. The 36 included Thomas Helyes who later returned to England and established the very first Baptist church in England. Later Smyth regarded his self-baptism as a mistake but it had already earned him the name of se-baptist meaning self baptist and later just Baptist as the name still stands even to this day.

Restoring the laver in such a dramatic way that drew attentlon, John Smythe was thus the founder of the Baptist movement. If I had been alive during his time, then I too would probably have been a Baptist.

May the knowledge of what changes were brought into the lives of people like John Smyth as they studied the Bible encourage you also to read the good book, the Bible.

21 WESLEY AND THE RESTORATION OF THE SANCTUARY

Let your light so shine before men, that they may see your good works, and glorify your Father which is in heaven. (Matthew 5:16)

In Epworth, England in the county of Linconshire in June 1703[9] was born a revivalist called John Wesley. He was a member of the church of England who, rather than wanting to come out of the church, intended to bring revival and reformation whilst remaining within. A graduate of Charterhouse and Christ Church of Oxford, Wesley sought to live and motivate others to live a righteous and devout Christian life.

What Wesley became well known for was his outdoor preaching and travels to take the gospel out and far into the world. This zeal for reaching out and sharing the good news about Jesus Christ effectively becomes a major part in the restoration of the 7 candlesticks in the sanctuary that Satan had knocked out. God was obviously behind Wesley's burden of sharing the message.

Wesley travelled and preached extensively across Great Britain and Ireland[10] and formed and

---

[9] https://en.wikipedia.org/wiki/John_Wesley
[10] https://en.wikipedia.org/wiki/John_Wesley

worked with Christian groups of ordinary laity who developed accountability to each other and helped each other grow. His methodology in organising the work of the gospel and the implementation of things such as prison reform and the abolition of slavery wrought the name of his movement which till this day is known as the Methodists.

Wesley encouraged a personal relationship with Jesus Christ for all people and hence a progression towards perfection. I consider that this was the correct thing to do as it is in tandem with Proverbs 4:18 which reads, "But the path of the just is as the shining light, that shineth more and more unto the perfect day." Christians should be growing better in their attitudes and progressively be developing spiritually as was taught by Wesley's methodism.

It goes without saying therefore that with the improvements that Wesley made upon the other reformers, it was time to evolve into a newer and even better understanding of the Bible as well as a practical application. Naturally this revival reformation movement would have had a large impact on the people of Wesley's day and ultimately made Wesley "the best loved man in England"[11]. I certainly would have probably

[11] https://en.wikipedia.org/wiki/John_Wesley

been part of the Methodist movement too if I had lived during Wesley's time.

God continued and continues to speak to people who read the Bible and to show them things that may not be so plain to see by others. It is important therefore to study the Bible to discover what else God has in store for his children, of whom we all are. May God's blessings be yours today and always.

22 MILLER AND THE RESTORATION OF THE SANCTUARY

"Behold, he cometh with clouds; and every eye shall see him, and they also which pierced him: and all kindreds of the earth shall wail because of him. Even so, Amen." (Revelation 1:7)

American born William Miller as a young man was fond of mocking Christians and their belief in God. He would imitate how they preached and cause entertainment by mocking them. He would laugh and cause others to laugh at how his father and how his uncle gestured while preaching.

As a grown up deist, Miller became an army lieutenant and later an army captain. During the war with Britain, Miller discovered that deism actually did not even believe in life beyond death. His deist friends compared life to a candle which burned until there was nothing left. He was now torn in two because he now had a problem with deism, and yet he also did not believe that the Bible was inspired.

The 1812 battle of Plattsburgh led Miller to question the deist doctrine that says that God does not intervene in man's affairs. He witnessed a small and outnumbered army that he was the captain of, defeating a British contingent that had just recently won a battle against Napoleon. He decided to return to his town of birth and attend the same Baptist church that he used to mock and laugh at his father and uncle from. He studied the scripture and decided to follow the chronological events that were in Daniel about 2300 days (Dan 8:14, 9:25) and the day for a year prophecies (Ezekiel 4:6 and Numbers 14:34).

In 1818, Miller, who was newly converted to Christianity, studied about the return of Jesus. He made a conclusion that not only would Christ return to earth, but that His return would take place as a visible and major event not as a secret or just a feeling as some people thought. (Matthew 25:31 & Matthew 24:23-27)

He carried out some calculations and concluded that Jesus would return to earth in 25 years. Based on the Karaite luni-solar calendar every Passover fell on a lunar weekly Sabbath. William Miller relied on this Lunar calculation to place the crucifixion in 31 AD. He calculated 2300 days/years from 457 BC via 31 AD through to 1844, so establishing 22 October 1844 as the day on which he believed that Jesus would return.

Miller was excited as this meant that all of earth's sorrows would soon be over. Soon, he thought, we were going to live with Jesus. The man was very happy for this. But he also felt anxious. He thought that

if Jesus was coming soon, then should he not tell everyone about it?
At first William Miller was reluctant but soon he realised that there was no time to waste. He began preaching so that as many people as possible would be ready to meet Jesus when He comes back. The ultimate result was the great disappointment as Jesus did not come in 1844 as Miller taught.
It was in the 1800s therefore that God used the Millerite movement to restore the ark of the covenant in the most holy place. After the great disappointment the group of people who comprised many different denominations restored the biblical Sabbath according to the 10 commandments which were in the most holy place of the sanctuary. After further Bible study they together formed the Seventh-day Adventist movement based on the belief that Jesus would return and that God had blessed the seventh day of the week as the Sabbath day and not Sunday. All Adventists are reformed Methodists, Baptists, Lutherans, Anglicans etc who came together to eventually establish a new church of Bible believing people who do not follow man's traditions but only Scripture. Of course this group of people is hated by Satan for trying to uphold God's commandments. Even among the Adventists are many sinners too who need a Saviour.

If there was any other movement that taught and kept the Bible any better then I would probably join them. But I believe that the Adventist beliefs are solidly biblical and thus I am a Seventh-day Adventist. May you study the Bible and in it find the truth from God and may this truth set you free. May God bless you and fill you with joy and peace today and always.

23 UNLOCKING THE KING'S DREAM

And wheresoever the children of men dwell, the beasts of the field and the fowls of the heaven hath he given into thine hand, and hath made thee ruler over them all. Thou art this head of gold. (Daniel 2:38)

We have looked at some historical accounts of church evolution through the centuries. We shall now turn to the Bible and consider a number of aspects and trace their developments and try to establish their significance and implications for this present day. Our end goal will be to see the prophecies given in the Bible and how they got fulfilled. We will also consider some world history to check if indeed what The Bible predicted would happen did happen.

We start our study from the book of Daniel and chapter 2. I strongly encourage you to read the entire book of Daniel. To follow my writing better and understand more clearly it is essential to read the story straight from the Bible (unless you know it already) because then otherwise I would have to reproduce it, and that is not ideal.

In case you have never heard the story I will give you a highlight. The story is about an ancient king who is troubled by a dream he has but which he has forgotten when he wakes up. He demands for his wise men and magicians to tell him his dream and also explain it. He threatens to kill them all unless they tell him the dream and its meaning. In the end Daniel, after praying to God, reveals both the dream and its interpretation. You have got to read this remarkable narrative for yourself in Daniel 2 in The Bible. You will be spellbound as you read this non-fiction story that contains the key to understanding history and the future. You would not want to be left out of this one.

From verse 37 Daniel explains the meaning of king Nebuchadnezzar's dream. The head of gold from the statue in the dream represents the kingdom of Babylon. Chapter 3 of the book of Daniel shows Nebuchadnezzar's ingenuity. He tries to go against the prophecy that was explained in Daniel 2. He is not satisfied that he is only the head. He wants to be the whole body of gold and to be worshipped too. Notwithstanding his brainchild genius ideas the prophecy does not change by him rejecting it.

The identity of Nebuchadnezzar being the head of gold was really nothing personal but national. It was not Nebuchadnezzar on the throne anymore but his grandson when the kingdom faced its demise.

Reading down to verse 45 of Daniel 2 gives much of what is now history as well as what must still happen. As the verse states, the things stated there will certainly happen. The fulfilment of the prophecy happens regardless of if we like it or not. It also happens regardless of if a king likes it or not, as was in Nebuchadnezzar's idea to change the prophecy to suit his liking.

As we proceed to unravel the prophecy further we shall also show the fulfilled aspects. I hope you are thrilled to journey into this path of historical investigation. May God bless you and fill you with joy today.

24 THE GOLDEN AGE OF BABYLON

Forasmuch as thou sawest that the stone was cut out of the mountain without hands, and that it brake in pieces the iron, the brass, the clay, the silver, and the gold; the great God hath made known to the king what shall come to pass hereafter: and the dream is certain, and the interpretation thereof sure. (Daniel 2:45)

When I lived Romania I met someone who told me an insider's story about the dictator of Romania's plans. As he showed me around the sturdy edifices in the capital city Bucharest with amazing architectural and historical significance he said the buildings were laid out in a way that was meant to write a statement. Apparently, if it had been completed, the aerial view of the statement would have been, "The Golden Age of Nicolae Ceausescu". Unfortunately for the project, Ceausescu was executed before fulfilling his ambition of marking his so-called golden age with buildings spelling text.

Gold is a mineral of wealth and prosperity. While Ceausescu desired to call his age the golden age of Romania, God Himself named the ancient Babylonian kingdom the kingdom of gold. Although some historians may not like to support the Biblical account in any way, they cannot change history or architecture to distort reality. That reality reveals to us the exact location and nature of Babylon.

Mesopotamia, known as "the land between" was located between the river Tigris and the river Euphrates. In Mesopotamia, was the city of Babylon through which the river Euphrates flowed. Babylon was discovered in excavations in the 19th century to be located in what is now modern Iraq[12]. National Geographic describes the "Golden age" of Babylon to have been during the 7th and 6th centuries B.C. Interestingly this is exactly the time that Daniel told Nebuchadnezzar that he was the head of gold in the statue in the dream (Daniel 2:38). The city of Babylon fell only in 539B.C. after being famous for its wealth and beauty. One of the most famous landmarks of wealth was the golden Ishtar Gate unearthed by German archaeologist Robert Koldewey. A reconstruction of the gate can be found even today at the Pergamon Museum in Berlin.

One of the most famous landscapes of the ancient world which was also known as one of the 7 wonders of the ancient world was "The Hanging Gardens"[13] which were found in Babylon. Using the spoils from other lands, Nebuchadnezzar had turned the city into a wonderful and admirable place of splendour. He even notoriously boasted about it immediately before he fulfilled a prophecy to become a beast, "The king spake, and said, Is not this great Babylon, that I have built for the house of the kingdom by the

---

12 https://www.nationalgeographic.com/history/magazine/2017/01-02/babylon-mesopotamia-ancient-city-iraq/

13 https://en.wikipedia.org/wiki/Hanging_Gardens_of_Babylon

might of my power, and for the honour of my majesty?" (Daniel 4:30).

Yet with all the lavish golden life of Babylon, the day of the end dawned on it one day. A new divided kingdom took over power, just as Daniel had explained in his interpretation of the dream to king Nebuchadnezzar. Indeed, as he had told the king, the dream was certain and interpretation sure. I encourage you to read your Bible not only for this particular prophecy but for the blessing and wisdom that can only come from God through the study of His word. Many blessings I pray unto you today.

25 THE TOWERING EVIDENCE

And they said, Go to, let us build us a city and a tower, whose top may reach unto heaven; and let us make us a name, lest we be scattered abroad upon the face of the whole earth. (Genesis 11:4)

The apparent incoherence of leaping from Daniel to Genesis may rightly raise your eyebrows at this point. What communion has the tower of Babel with Daniel? You may wonder. There is a lot more commonality than we will be able to examine with brevity. Sufficeth it to say that the name Babylon by itself should sound like Babel to anyone, without a stretch of their auditory skills. Then add to that the fact that Daniel's interaction with kings occurs in Babylon. I am sure you already clearly get the association. In Genesis 11 verse 9, the Hebrew word for "confused" is babal, which sounds like babel (Babylon). The great evil of the tower builders is their sinful pride against the rule of God. This theme of evil reappears numerous times in the prophetic writings of the Bible against the city of Babylon. A number of historical artefacts exist to support the authenticity of the Bible.

In 2017 Andrew George, a professor of Babylonia at the University of London was reported to have found solid evidence for the tower of Babel in an ancient baked tablet from the city of Babylon. Separately but yet significantly, according to livius.org the best description of the monumental tower can be found in a cuneiform tablet from Uruk, written in 229 BC. It is a copy of an older text and is now in the Louvre in Paris. It states that the tower was made up of seven terraces and it gives the height of the seven stocks - 91 metres all in all. These are very significant elements of history that give credibility to what some have dismissed as fables in the Bible.

The British Museum in London is home to some 5000 years old 130,000 Assyrian cuneiform tablets. One of them names Nabu-sharrusu-kin who in Jeremiah 39:3 is given as king Nebuchadnezzar's chief eunuch.

The narrative given in Daniel 5 that Nebuchadnezzar was living with animals for 7 years is also supported in an indirect way by archaeology. The fact that between 582 and 575 BC there are no decrees or acts at all that were signed by king Nebuchadnezzar

implyingly support that the king indeed suffered from a mental illness as the Bible says.

Those who avoid the Bible as a fallacy must face up to the fact that history keeps showing up with proof that the Bible is true. I hope you are motivated to read the Bible for yourself and then enjoy archaeology that helps bring out the truth of the Bible.

26 A 66 CUBIT HIGH GOD

Our God whom we serve is able to deliver us from the burning fiery furnace, and he will deliver us out of thine hand, O king. But if not, be it known unto thee, O king, that we will not serve thy gods, nor worship the golden image which thou hast set up. (Daniel 3:17-18)

I still have a few more things to share with you but I hope by now you have confidence in your Bible and that the stories we are referring to are not just fictional stories. Yet I invite you to indulge me a bit as I use my imagination in reading the account of the image of gold and the furnace. I strongly advise you to read the story from the Bible, minus my comments, to receive your own edification.

After hearing the accurate and sure description of his dream as well as what Daniel emphasises as a certain future application for the dream, Nebuchadnezzar obviously feels troubled by the prospect of an imminent loss of his cherished empire. His brain sets off to work and he desires to be like the most high God and receive worship. His game changing strategy is building the six cubit tall image of gold.

The height of the image itself is most probably just a coincidence but yet for me fits the description of attaining the inferiority of man's best. Given that, of necessity, this is a god to be worshipped, the best shot by Nebuchadnezzar immediately gives the statue the mark of a man which, as I read, is synonymous with the mark of the beast. Even though it had been 77 it would still have been inferior as it is just but an image. Yet the number 66 association just makes it a fascinating choice. But it certainly is not the 666 that Revelation warns about.

The three Hebrews refuse to bow down and are brought directly to the king for cross-examination and judgement. Note that Nebuchadnezzar ends his warning to Shadreck, Misheck and Abednego by asking "Who is that God that shall deliver you out of my hands?" (Daniel 3:15) He seems to have forgotten about the God who revealed the meaning of the dream to him in the previous chapter. We shall consider a little more on this apparent amnesia shortly. Before that let us focus a little more on the golden image of false worship and the fire prepared for those who decline to participate in the false worship that is not of God.

Searching for any archaeological finds of the image has not yielded any desirable results for me. Yet what I did find however is information about how executions by fire were commonplace in Babylon. That suggests that Nebuchadnezzar's plan to punish dissent by the fiery furnace could be considered.normal for his era. His rage however to order the furnace to deliver seven times it's normal heat misses the aspect of delivering maximum torture that could be achieved by burning slowly.

It turns out that those who participated in trying to enforce the false worship are the ones who were engulfed and quickly consumed by the flames in the furnace. The Bible speaks of hell fire prepared for Satan and his angels (Matthew 25:41) not for people. Interestingly the fire of hell is a consuming fire that obliterates quickly not slowly as would be a fire intended to torture. It's burning forever means the effects of the burning are eternal. Sodom and Gomora were also said to burn forever but they are not burning anymore, yet forever fire was used to eliminate them.

Let us now come back to the question the apparently amnesia stricken king Nebuchadnezzar asked about what God would save the Hebrews from fire. I am intrigued that nobody is needed to tell the king who the fourth person in the fire is. Suddenly the king turns into a preacher calling his counsellors to see the one who he says is like the Son of God. The Hebrews were flung into the furnace bound but with the Son of God they were free and walking.

The Bible will never fail to affect those who diligently study it and who do so prayerfully and with humility not pomp. Give it a try, pray to God and study it for yourself and receive your own personal and unique experience of blessings. God bless you.

27 THE WRITING IS ON THE WALL

In the same hour came forth fingers of a man's hand, and wrote over against the candlestick upon the plaister of the wall of the king's palace: and the king saw the part of the hand that wrote. (Daniel 5:5)

In chapter 5 of the book of Daniel we find the grandson of king Nebuchadnezzar now the reigning monarch. Not only is he a wild party animal but he has no regard for God's Holy property. Or perhaps he does not understand that the God of the Israelites is the almighty creator God who has shown Himself over and over to king Nebuchadnezzar. I think he will have either seen or at least heard of the miracles experienced by Nebuchadnezzar and of the dreams he had heard. Certainly the king' s 7 years of living with wild animals in fulfilment of the dream as explained by Daniel were well known to him (verse 22).

The Bible says that Belshazzar made a feast for a thousand people. Among the people at the feast were his princes, wives and concubines. Then while he was getting drunk he ordered that the golden and silver vessels from the temple in Jerusalem be brought to him. Whatever motive he has for doing this is not given. But it is certainly not because he has run out of his own vessels to drink from. Most probably he just wants to spite the God of Israel and show off his own greatness before the gathered multitude. He wants to show off to his wives and concubines.

As the wild party continues, while drinking wine from God's vessels all the guests join the king in (Daniel 5:4) praising the gods of gold, and of silver, of brass, of iron, of wood, and of stone. Then the king gets a rude awakening (for want of a better expression) as a bodiless hand appears and writes on the wall before his eyes.

Notice something interesting here. Belshazzar and his subjects are the only ones ever to experience the writing literally being on the real wall. The expression derived from this historic event is used for depicting many situations that apply in the same, albeit less significant, manner. Yet many refuse to read the Bible from which the expression comes.

When the real writing is on the wall the king's knees smite against each other (verse 6) and the king cries out loud for help (verse 7). When the writing is on the wall, the party is over and panic is the natural reaction for a godless person. The old queen comes in and finds the chaotic situation but she remains calm. She counsels the king to stay calm and send for Daniel who, as he comes in, is not panic stricken either. Hence panicking, in this account is just for the uninformed and the ungodly.

See if by reading your Bible you may find this to be true: panicking is for the uninformed and the ungodly. Think about if this is applicable today and to all the situations that the people of the world are facing, even now. May God bless you as you ponder over these words. And may your day be filled with blessings. "Be still and know that I am God" (Psalm 46:10).

28 PROPHECY FULFILLED, CONFIRMED BY HISTORY

And this is the writing that was written, MENE, MENE, TEKEL, UPHARSIN.
(Daniel 5:25)

The meaning of the statue image dream of king Nebuchadnezzar was not fulfilled in his lifetime. It was not even fulfilled when Nabonidas was king but only when Belshazzar the grandson of Nebuchadnezzar was the king. This point is of extreme importance because many prophecies given as warnings to people in the Bible have been ignored. People have paid the price of losing their lives when prophecies were eventually fulfilled.

Noah' s ark ended up with just Noah's family because people refused to believe the prophecy, even as they saw animals getting into the ark. Jerusalem was destroyed and Israel taken captive for not taking heed of prophetic warnings. Daniel chastised the king for not acting any wiser in spite of having full awareness of the prophecies given to his grandfather king Nebuchadnezzar.

As he read and explained to Belshazzar, "MENE MENE TERKEL URPHASIN" Daniel was talking to a trading merchant. As a merchant, Belshazzar understood about measuring on a balance very well. What he did not realise was that Babylon as the head of gold was about to fall that very night even as his own life was just about to end.

In fulfilment of prophecy, the Medes and Persians took Babylon under Cyrus the Great and the kingdom was divided just as Daniel had told Nebuchadnezzar it would. History proves all these things without any involvement of Scripture.

The Bible is disregarded by many as irrelevant. Many think and say that the Bible is out of date. Yet from the Bible we learn that God is the same today as He was yesterday and He will be the same forever. Read your Bible and experience His love and mercy for yourself. God bless you as you read.

29 THE BRASS BELLY AND THIGHS

And now will I shew thee the truth. Behold, there shall stand up yet three kings in Persia; and the fourth shall be far richer than they all: and by his strength through his riches he shall stir up all against the realm of Grecia. And a mighty king shall stand up, that shall rule with great dominion, and do according to his will. (Daniel 11:2-3)

Following his conquest of Babylon, Cyrus had built the Medo-Persian empire that included Babylon as a province. Cyrus had freed the Jewish people from Babylonian captivity and allowed them to return to Jerusalem and was well loved for that. We shall speak more about him in a different section later in our discourse.

The battle against Alexander the Great spelled the fall of Medo-Persia in 330 B.C. Thus was the fulfilment of the prophecy given as a dream to Nebuchadrezzar according to Daniel's exact explanation. Alexander the Great was born in 356 B.C., almost 200 years after the book of Daniel was written in 535 B.C. In Daniel 11 and verses 2 and 3 there is a description of how the Persian empire could not push back against Greece and how it was eventually conquered by a mighty Greek king. Daniel chapter 8 verse 21 gives even more details about this great Greek king.

Although the Bible does not mention Alexander by name it does mention Grecia which is Greece. Greece was therefore represented by the brass belly and thighs of the image in king Nebuchadrezzar's dream. How remarkable that the Bible had predicted centuries before, and with such precision, what is now history.

May you be inspired to read the Bible and as you do, may you be blessed.

30 THE IRON LEGS

And the fourth kingdom shall be strong as iron: forasmuch as iron breaketh in pieces and subdueth all things: and as iron that breaketh all these, shall it break in pieces and bruise. (Daniel 2:40)

The brass kingdom of Greece led by Alexander the Great came to an end. The next kingdom as Daniel 2:40 says would be as strong as iron that would break into pieces and bruise whatever was in its way. It was centuries before the kingdom would arise that its characteristics were described to Nebuchadrezzar following his dream, Enter pagan Rome.

The Roman Empire will always be remembered as one of the toughest kingdoms in history. It will also always be remembered as one of the most cruel and bloodthirsty kingdoms. The Romans even invented entertainment in which crowds of thousands would watch and cheer while people were being brutally killed. For example, as stated by Cristin O'Keefe Aptowicz, "To keep the Roman crowds happy and engaged by bloodshed, bestiarii were forced to consistently invent new ways to kill. They devised elaborate contraptions and platforms to give prisoners the illusion they could save themselves — only to have the structures collapse at the worst possible moments, dropping the condemned into a waiting pack of starved animals. Prisoners were tied to boxes, lashed to stakes, wheeled out on dollies and nailed to crosses, and then, prior to the animals' release, the action was paused so that bets could be made in the crowd about which of the helpless men would be devoured first."[14]

Additionally, the Roman Empire was ruthless in its invasion of other nations. In the words of Joshua Munguti, "In the reign of the Roman Empire, in 70 AD the Romans come down into Israel, destroyed the temple, slaughtered many people, raped women, wiped out everything and every person and all Jews were scattered all over the world." [15]

Before the Roman Empire even came to exist with Augustus Caesar declaring himself the emperor of Rome, the Bible had already outlined how it would be. It would be a kingdom that would break to pieces and bruise. That is exactly how the empire was. The Bible reveals many things that many people do not know about. If only they would read it! I hope you are motivated to search and learn from the Bible for yourself. May God bless you as you study the Bible.

---

[14] https://www.livescience.com/author/cristin-okeefe-aptowicz

[15] https://www.christiantruthcenter.com/nebuchadnezzars-dream/

31 THEY SHALL NOT CLEAVE ONE TO ANOTHER

And whereas thou sawest iron mixed with miry clay, they shall mingle themselves with the seed of men: but they shall not cleave one to another, even as iron is not mixed with clay. (Daniel 2:43)

May I implore you, if you will, to walk into the royal residence of the Habsburg monarchs. Into this magnificent 1,441-room Schönbrunn Palace in Hietzing, Vienna, Austria is where I want you to focus your mind as you imagine this huge building standing on and surrounded by amazingly beautiful gardens and historical information that you can experience within the place and go back as far as over 300 years.

Feel with me the hair-raising experience of entering into the very bedroom of the Holy Roman Empress Maria Theresa Walburga Amalia Christina who was the sovereign of Austria, Hungary, Croatia, Bohemia, Transylvania, Mantua, Milan, Lodomeria and Galicia, the Austrian Netherlands, and Parma (1745-1765). The tension of reading, right inside the palace, just how Maria Theresa's own children were forced into marriages for the political benefit of the state and against their own happiness is just inescapable and surreal. For instance, Maria Theresa's daughter, Maria Antonia Josepha Johanna who was born on 2nd November 1755 was married at 14 to Louis-Auguste the heir apparent to the French throne. She later became the last Queen of France before the French Revolution when her husband was now king Louis XVI.

I begin to feel my heart beat as I realise for the first time that I am right inside a place that reminds me of a verse in the Bible that I only knew the theory of but that I never imagined could make me happy to be exploring such a place. Palaces and castles never brought me any excitement before my sojourn to Eastern European countries. My wife takes the credit for dragging me almost kicking and screaming into places I had no idea would forever impact me and influence how I look at history and reflect on what is in the Bible. This particular experience I am relating now is happening in December of 2016. I beg your pardon for coming out of it, let us go back into it now.

The text that says "they shall mingle themselves with the seed of men" suddenly comes to mind as I realise how that process went on. The intermarrying of the Habsburgs is not the only manifestation of the mingling of the seed of men. There are a myriad of others such as Francis II who was the king of France from 1559 to 1560. Francis II was also king consort of Scotland as a result of his marriage to Mary, Queen of Scots.

The intermarriages did not completely prevent wars in Europe and neither did it produce a permanent cementation of relations. Several different political arrangements were attempted and even till this day continue being attempted to keep the nations together. The European Union is just one such example of these efforts to keep Europe united for political and economic reasons. Yet as what has now become known as Brexit shows the text to remain true, "they shall not cleave one to another, even as iron is not mixed with clay".

This brings us to the very feet and toes of the statue dreamt by king Nebuchadnezzar. We can now be certain that any unity that appears to be in place will never last because if the Bible can be trusted (which so far you can be certain that it can) then there will never be an endless union. As iron cannot be mixed with clay, the nations will never be permanently bonded and united. While for now the statue is still standing, we know it needs to be smashed by a stone. We shall look into the stone next but in the meantime, remain blessed as you read your Bible.

32 THE STONE CUT WITHOUT HANDS

Forasmuch as thou sawest that the stone was cut out of the mountain without hands, and that it brake in pieces the iron, the brass, the clay, the silver, and the gold; the great God hath made known to the king what shall come to pass hereafter: and the dream is certain, and the interpretation thereof sure. (Daniel 2:45)

As Daniel concludes his interpretation of the king's dream he says that "And in the days of these kings shall the God of heaven set up a kingdom, which shall never be destroyed: and the kingdom shall not be left to other people, but it shall break in pieces and consume all these kingdoms, and it shall stand for ever."(Daniel 2:45) The end of the kingdoms of the earth that are failing to cleave to one another will be brought by the setting up of the new kingdom that the God of heaven will set up. Revelation 11:15 says, "The kingdoms of this world are become the kingdoms of our Lord, and of his Christ; and he shall reign for ever and ever."

As Nebuchadnezzar saw in his dream, a stone coming from the mountain without any hands it is worth noting that Jesus is sometimes depicted in the Bible as a stone. So the return of Jesus to bring earth's history to a close is depicted as a stone coming from the mountain. "Wherefore also it is contained in the scripture, Behold, I lay in Sion a chief corner stone, elect, precious: and he that believeth on him shall not be confounded." (1 Peter 2:6)

Interestingly, where the stone comes from is referred to as from the mountain. This is in line with several references that depict God as being in the mountain. Several times Moses went to the mountain to communicate with God. “And Moses went up unto God, and the Lord called unto him out of the mountain.” (Exodus 19:3) The ten commandments were given to Moses when He went up to meet God in the mountain.

In the book of Isaiah the house of the Lord is in the mountains. “And it shall come to pass in the last days, that the mountain of the LORD'S house shall be established in the top of the mountains, and shall be exalted above the hills; and all nations shall flow unto it.” (Isaiah 2:2) Again there is reference to God’s holy mountain in the book of Isaiah: “Even them will I bring to my holy mountain, and make them joyful in my house of prayer: their burnt offerings and their sacrifices shall be accepted upon mine altar; for mine house shall be called an house of prayer for all people.” (Isaiah 56:7)

If all the earlier prophecies given in the book of Daniel 2 have been fulfilled, then we can expect the rest to also be fulfilled. We therefore need to diligently study the word of God to understand even more about other things that He wants us to know and discover how He wants us to be. As we study more we will realise that the time is now running out and we need to get ready for Jesus’ second coming. I hope you will now study your Bible and get ready to meet the creator of the universe.

Be blessed as you study!

33 JESUS AND CYRUS PARALLELS

That saith of Cyrus, He is my shepherd, and shall perform all my pleasure: even saying to Jerusalem, Thou shalt be built; and to the temple, Thy foundation shall be laid. (Isaiah 44:28)

We now return to focus slightly more on Cyrus the great. His grandfather was King Astyages of the Medes. Herodotus the credible Greek historian records the legend[16] that Astyages had a dream before Cyrus was born. He dreamt that out of his daughter Mandane flowed a stream of water that flooded all of Asia. Astyages asked his interpreters the meaning of the dream.

The interpreters told the king that his daughter would have a son who would overthrow his rule. To prevent this, the king sent his trusted servant Harpagus to kill & bury his daughter's child as soon as he was born. Harpagus could not stand the thought of killing the newborn - so he gave him to a shepherd and his wife to kill him.

The shepherd and his wife however could not bear the idea of killing him neither. So, concludes the legend, they raised him as their own child. Thus around 590 BC, Cyrus was born in Southwest Iran. Cyrus was born to fulfil the prophecy

---

16 https://www.ducksters.com/history/mesopotamia/cyrus_the_great.php

in Isaiah 44:28 (see also Isaiah 45:1). So, 150 years before he was even born, Cyrus was named in the Bible.

Now consider Matthew 2:12-13, 16. "And being warned of God in a dream that they should not return to Herod, they departed into their own country another way. And when they were departed, behold, the angel of the Lord appeareth to Joseph in a dream, saying, Arise, and take the young child and his mother, and flee into Egypt, and be thou there until I bring thee word: for Herod will seek the young child to destroy him. Then Herod, when he saw that he was mocked of the wise men, was exceeding wroth, and sent forth, and slew all the children that were in Bethlehem, and in all the coasts thereof, from two years old and under, according to the time which he had diligently enquired of the wise men."

So Jesus was born in Bethlehem of Judaea according to the prophecy. Jesus was born to save people from their sins and to give them liberty. Cyrus liberated the Jews from Babylonian captivity.

More about Cyrus will be discussed next but with the brief highlight of the resemblance of Cyrus's story to that of Jesus I hope you are moved to study your Bible. God bless you.

34 BABYLON AND RIVER EUPHRATES

Set up the standard upon the walls of Babylon, make the watch strong, set up the watchmen, prepare the ambushes: for the Lord hath both devised and done that which he spake against the inhabitants of Babylon. O thou that dwellest upon many waters, abundant in treasures, thine end is come, and the measure of thy covetousness. (Jeremiah 51:12-13)

We have previously referred to the Cyrus Cylinder which is displayed in the British Museum in London, England. On the Cyrus Cylinder text, clearly inscribed in Babylonian cuneiform are words about the night of the Babylonian conquest which read, "Cyrus' troops strolled along, their weapons packed away, without any battle entered the city of Babylon and spared Babylon any damage." In Daniel 5, the Bible speaks of the great feast that king Belshazaar was having when Cyrus and his troops invaded and took over Babylon.

The Euphrates river in the Old Testament, is called "the great river". Genesis 15:18 says, "In the same day the Lord made a covenant with Abram, saying, Unto thy seed have I given this land, from the river of Egypt unto the great river, the river Euphrates." Also Deuteronomy 1:7 and Joshua 1:4 both call it "the great river". Euphrates river is the boundary that separated God's people from their enemies Assyria and Babylon. It was the place from which the archenemy nations would invade Israel.

Jeremiah 1:63-64 tells us that ancient Babylon was situated on the river Euphrates. The river ran through the city and allowed cargo ships to enter the city for trade. There were 2 spiked gates at either side of the river at the entrance and exit of Babylon. It was an integral part of the city, nurturing its crops and providing water for the city's inhabitants. Without that river, Babylon could not survive. A wealthy city had a river in it or near it. In Daniel 4:30, "Is not this great Babylon that I have built?' king Nebuchadnezzar bragged. But yet according to Isaiah 44:27 God had said, "I will dry up thy rivers".

As stated before, when Cyrus conquered Babylon, Israel was delivered from captivity. Like Christ, Cyrus delivered God's remnant people as the great deliverer for whom they had long waited. The usage of the phrase "my anointed Cyrus" in Isaiah 45:1 is significant because in Hebrew it means "my messiah" and the Greek form of this term means Christ. Additionally, Isaiah 48:28 calls Cyrus "My Shepherd" which is a messianic title. Therefore Cyrus is depicted as a type or symbol of Christ.

The book of Revelation 17:1 states that the prostitute Babylon sits on many waters. Also, Jeremiah 51:13 shows that the expression "many waters" by which Babylon was located is another reference to the Euphrates river.

There have been quite a bit of Bible cross-references in today's brief reading. Please re-visit them in your own Bible and study them and do a thorough cross-check to see if you can understand and follow them because next we will examine where or who Babylon is in our modern times. May you be blessed as you study and reflect.

35 MODERN BABYLON

"Come hither; I will shew unto thee the judgment of the great whore that sitteth upon many waters: With whom the kings of the earth have committed fornication, and the inhabitants of the earth have been made drunk with the wine of her fornication." (Revelation 17:1-2)

Before we consider the fall of Babylon it is worth considering what the Bible says about Babylon so, hopefully, we will have no doubt about who is being referred to. There are many interpretations out there which can be misleading and leave people confused. Let us discover what the Bible says about it and pray we can bring out a useful meaning even in brevity.

The 18th verse of Revelation 17 shows that Babylon is in effect a great city that rules over the kings of the earth. In fact chapter 17 of Revelation gives many clues that can help to identify the woman called Babylon, which is not a literal woman but a city which essentially must be a religious body to be referred to as a woman and yet with political power to be able to influence different kings or rulers of countries.

Babylon has children who can be identified. The identity of the children of Babylon is by the mark on their foreheads which has the name of the beast, "And that no man might buy or sell, save he that had the mark, or the name of the beast, or the number of his name." This is a sharp contrast from the children of the woman in Revelation

12 who stand with the lamb and are "an hundred forty and four thousand, having his Father's name written in their foreheads." (Revelation 14:1)

The attire of Babylon, purple and scarlet and precious stones and gold is remarkably similar to that of the Old Testament high priest officiating in the sanctuary services as described in Exodus 28. A search for the attires of priests, bishops and cardinals of modern religious bodies may help find who modern Babylon is to be sure.

Revelation 13:14-17 shows that Babylon has for so long been persecuting the saints that she is now drunk from their blood. I leave it with you, dear reader to decide just who fits into this description. From Revelation 17 we can see the combination or alliance of the dragon, earth beast and sea beast to become Babylon the great.

A deeper study of the Bible with diligent prayer would do better justice to the subject than what we have covered today. Nonetheless I hope you now have a greater appetite to read the Bible to understand. God bless you as you read.

36 THE EUPHRATES RIVER IS DRYING UP

And Moses stretched out his hand over the sea; and the Lord caused the sea to go back by a strong east wind all that night, and made the sea dry land, and the waters were divided. And the children of Israel went into the midst of the sea upon the dry ground: and the waters were a wall unto them on their right hand, and on their left. (Exodus 14:21-22)

The angel explains to John in Revelation 17:15 that the waters upon which the prostitute Babylon sits symbolise the national powers of this world - i.e, peoples, and multitudes and nations and tongues. “And he saith unto me, The waters which thou sawest, where the whore sitteth, are peoples, and multitudes, and nations, and tongues.”(Revelation 17:15) These national powers of this world are the ones who will end time, Babylon and its opposition to God and His people.

So ancient Babylon was just like modern Babylon. Just as the rich and prosperous religious and political and economic systems of the modern world are busy partying and reaching out for the vessels from the temple, a hand appears on the wall. The economic system is already under serious threat. People are beginning to realise the illusion of the financial systems. The currency used in most countries is no longer even backed by mineral resources. They are just printing money and running countries deeper into debt.

Governments are borrowing money by the trillions and calling it quantitative easing of economic problems.

There are trade wars currently going on coupled with sanctions and threats of sanctions again countries. Some countries are not only threatening to but have taken steps to significantly eliminate doing their business and trade using the American dollar. Global pandemic and lockdown conditions are at an unprecedented scale and will undoubtedly change the lives of people forever with the re-introduction of movement restrictions and the introduction of the so-called social distancing measures.

There is talk of avoiding the use of cash altogether and using card payment systems. At the same time with many people forcibly stopped to work, financial systems of entire countries are under threat. Speaking of end times, Revelation 16:12 says "the sixth angel poured out his vial upon the great river Euphrates; and the water thereof was dried up". The wealth of the city of Babylon depended on the river Euphrates. Judgement is upon Babylon now.

If you study Revelation 17 and 18 you will see that modern Babylon is about to receive the same judgement as did ancient Babylon. Please take time to read the two chapters of Revelation 17 and 18 before we look at the final battle of Armageddon. May God bless you as you read.

37 ARMAGEDDON IS COMING

Behold, I come as a thief. Blessed is he that watcheth, and keepeth his garments, lest he walk naked, and they see his shame.
And he gathered them together into a place called in the Hebrew tongue Armageddon. (Revelation 16:15-16)

I grew up hearing lots of different things about Armageddon. It was such a fearful place that I pictured in my mind. The fear was compounded by the fact that the word was always referred to as associated with a battle. My understanding did not improve very much all through most of my life because I never bothered myself much about the subject. So I never really studied much or read much to become enlightened.

It turns out that Megido, from which the word Armageddon is derived, is just a little mound hill that can hardly even be called a hill. My professor R. Stefanovic told us of an archaeological tour with some of his students from Andrews University to the Middle East.

He spoke of how each of them wanted to go and see the mount of Armageddon. When they were in the right place where it should have been, they were very disappointed to learn that it does not even exist!

Like the battle at mount Carmel was a spiritual issue about who God is - Armageddon is a battle, a spiritual battle in which all the people of the earth must give allegiance either to God or to Satan!

But thank God that we have a hope that Christ is coming to deliver us from the grips of destruction that will come over Babylon at the battle of Armageddon. Yes, God will win the final battle of Armageddon. We are blessed in that we can read the end of the Bible and appreciate how the end shall come. Be blessed as you continue to read your Bible and may you hear God speaking to you.

38 WARNING, PERSECUTION COMING

And that no man might buy or sell, save he that had the mark, or the name of the beast, or the number of his name. (Revelation 13:17)

At a time when everyone is fed up of global pandemics (either man made or natural it does not even matter), the earth and nature are observed to benefit. Global carbon foot-prints are at an all time low. Heavy industry plants have been shut down. Tourism has been closed and the aviation sector brought to a halt. Driving cars has been minimised as people are compelled to stay at home. So air pollution is drastically reduced. The skies are clearer as no industrial smoke is rising. Wildlife is now roaming more freely though more in danger as crossing quieter roads can still be futile for it. More birds can be seen than before and their singing is more pronounced.

There are people who have a vested interest in the situation of peace and calm seen in the environment. They have wanted to enforce religious Sunday observance by law for centuries. They have in fact attempted making such legislation in the past and it fell through because protestants were really and truly still protesting against unbiblical practices of the church and protestants were still keen students of the Bible.

Now ecumenism is the buzz word and unity is sought after without so much consideration of any deeper and future implications. This unity is fast approaching the point of restoring political and religious power to the very seat that was protested against. Unitedly, under one religious leader they will decide to keep a sacred day, namely Sunday as a day of worship and rest for the benefit of the environment. You will recall that change to the sacredness of Sunday was stated by the papacy to be their mark of authority as a church. You may also be aware that all protestants called the papacy the beast and the anti-Christ (research it more for yourself). "Anti" also means "in place of", which means the same as vicar.

So the result of the alliance of churches will be the passing of laws to enforce Sunday observance and death decrees against the few who resist. Just as they were pushing governments to enforce lockdowns for covid-19, the widely circular world population will support these laws as a necessary sacrifice to save the world. Armageddon, like mount Camel, comes to test the allegiance of the people. Whose side you choose either saves you from worldly trouble (albeit for a very short time before the plagues in the book of Revelation come) or puts you knowingly and directly against obeying God. There is no neutral ground and you are judged by what knowledge you have. God is kind and merciful and even now is bringing you understanding so you will recognise things as they unfold.

In spite of all the persecution, God's people will remain steadfast because they know He will deliver them (for my reader's comprehension, the expression God's people shall have the last laugh comes to mind but is contextually inappropriate). Read your Bible more for better understanding and particularly Isaiah 26:20-21 which ends, "the Lord cometh out of his place to punish the inhabitants of the earth for their iniquity." May God remain with you now and always.

39 THE SEAL OR MARK

"And there followed another angel, saying, Babylon is fallen, is fallen, that great city, because she made all nations drink of the wine of the wrath of her fornication."
(Revelation 14:8)

In concluding the events of earth's history there will only be two categories of people. The one group will have accepted the mark of the beast and consciously and willingly continued to reject the 4th commandment. The Bible states that when one is guilty of violating one commandment they are guilty of violating all. The other group will have the seal of God.

I find it rather fascinating to think that man will try to destroy those who reject the mark of the beast while God will inevitably destroy those who choose to go with the beast and God will also destroy the beast itself.

The destruction of the wicked will include those who trivialise God's commands and compromise by choosing for themselves to say some commandments are not so important. The Sabbath will still be kept even in heaven. So if God has said it is important to remember to keep his Sabbath holy and the Bible states that in heaven the Sabbath will still be there (Isaiah 66:23) then why would we choose to follow man's ideas? To question the commandment given by God sounds to me very much like Satan creating doubt in Eve's mind by asking her "did God really say..?"

The call to come out of Babylon is not only a call to come out of false worship. It is also an earnest plea to come out of destruction. By the level of our knowledge and understanding will be our judgement given. Unto whom much is given, much is required.

It is not legalism to keep God's commandment but obedience. In John 14:15 Jesus says, "If you love me, keep my commandments." He does not give exceptions of any of the 10 commandments. Some say the only commandments Jesus gave are to love God and to love man. If you re-examine the 10 commandments you will find that the first 4 are about loving God and the rest are about loving fellow mankind. If we can pick and choose which commandments to keep then some who like to steal for instance, could exclude obeying the commandment that forbids stealing.

The experience of the joy and blessing of keeping the Sabbath, like the joy of being a parent, cannot be described and explained to another. Only personal experience of it can help to understand why the Sabbath was made for man and not man for the Sabbath as the Bible declares. My simple logic tells me that if you knowingly refuse to keep God's Sabbath now then heaven is not a choice place for you.

Please study your Bible with an open mind about the seal of God found in Revelation 7:2. As always, May you be blessed as you study The Word of God.

40 GOD'S COMMANDMENTS OR MAN'S REASON

And the Spirit and the bride say, Come. And let him that heareth say, Come. And let him that is athirst come. And whosoever will, let him take the water of life freely. (Revelation 22:17)

As a conclusion it is worth reflecting a little about what is at stake. God says that He changes not. Jesus declares that heaven and earth may pass away but not one jot of the law shall pass away. So it is worth examining the credibility of the source of change to God's unchanging law. Only Satan could be behind it since it was he who first became disgruntled with God's government.

Remember that for a counterfeit to work, the one on whom it is used must be deceived and believe it to be genuine. Satan works in smart and crafty ways and he is said in the Bible to be like a roaring lion trying to devour anyone he can and if possible to deceive even the very elect. So just because the majority of the world is deceived does not change God's truth. The truth is never the most popular and anyway humanist philosophers have now convinced people that truth is both relative and subjective. They say everyone can have their own truth! Jesus says "I am the way, the truth and the life." Study about Jesus and from him you will learn the absolute truth well enough to spot the counterfeits.

Does this mean that all who are deceived will be destroyed? Not at all. The Lord knows what is in their hearts. He knows who is genuinely deceived and who is stubbornly refusing counsel and correction. He does say that he has "other sheep" who are not in His fold. Some may never even hear of the Sabbath truth but they remain good God's children. They just will not experience the Sabbath till they get to heaven. But for those who learn of it and still refuse to obey. Christ pleads with them to harden not their hearts. The blessed Sabbath experience was made for God's people and it is a delightful and refreshing blessing. Yet refusing to obey when you believe and understand can be futile. The Sabbath was made before the Jews and the law of God was there too even for Adam and Eve, just not on a stone tablet.

As you watch the world using pandemics to tamper with God's law and as you watch them introducing regulations to enforce Sunday worship under the guise of rest, family time and benefits to the environment, please note what you have learned. Will you knowingly accept the mark of the beast just because it is the easy way out?

May God's angels attend you as you study your Scriptures. May you find peace in the decisions you make. God appeals to your intellect and invites you and says, "Come let us reason together." His invitation is for you and for "whosoever will".

41 LET THE RIVER DRY UP

And the children of Israel went into the midst of the sea upon the dry ground: and the waters were a wall unto them on their right hand, and on their left. (Exodus 14:22)

When Cyrus overthrew Babylon, the first thing he did was divert the river Euphratess so it would not flow into Babylon anymore. Babylon could not stand without its river that gave it protection. The king and his nobles were feasting and enjoying their lives as the Euphrates river was drying up. The river had to be dry for the redemption of the Israelites to occur.

So if we see that the river Euphrates is really drying up, what does that do to us? Please do not despair because it is a good thing for it to dry up. When the river dries up you should lift up your hands because it means your redemption is drawing nigh. Only the oppressors of God's people should be terrified of the judgement that comes with the drying up of the river.

We have all the reasons to rejoice because the drying up of waters in the Old Testament often symbolises a mighty action of God on behalf of His people. (Exodus 14:21-22) Take a good look at Joshua 3:14-17 which says,

> "And it came to pass, when the people removed from their tents, to pass over Jordan, and the priests

> bearing the ark of the covenant before the people; And as they that bare the ark were come unto Jordan, and the feet of the priests that bare the ark were dipped in the brim of the water, (for Jordan overfloweth all his banks all the time of harvest,) That the waters which came down from above stood and rose up upon an heap very far from the city Adam, that is beside Zaretan: and those that came down toward the sea of the plain, even the salt sea, failed, and were cut off: and the people passed over right against Jericho. And the priests that bare the ark of the covenant of the Lord stood firm on dry ground in the midst of Jordan, and all the Israelites passed over on dry ground, until all the people were passed clean over Jordan."

Yes, Christ the king of kings riding with the armies of heaven is coming to deliver us and put an end to Babylon and all the forces that support it. He is coming to make us walk on dry ground as He did for the Israelites.

Just as the fall of ancient Babylon which oppressed God's people resulted in their deliverance and return to their homeland, the fall of modern Babylon which oppresses God's people will also result in their deliverance and their being taken home to heaven. Let us all make a choice to be on God's side not on the side of the enemies of the cross. Hell fire was meant for Satan and his angels, not for God's people.

So, let us keep all our hope alive and burning within our hearts. Keep up your hope in the coming of the Lord and keep reading your Bible! Amen!

www.ingramcontent.com/pod-product-compliance
Lightning Source LLC
LaVergne TN
LVHW012111160826
845678LV00014B/3045

* 9 7 8 6 0 6 9 7 2 3 1 1 1 *